EXPLORING COUNTRIES

COSTA RICA

Tracy Vonder Brink

TABLE OF CONTENTS

A Crabtree Seedlings Book

Crabtree Publishing
crabtreebooks.com

School-to-Home Support for Caregivers and Teachers

This book helps children grow by letting them practice reading. Here are a few guiding questions to help the reader with building his or her comprehension skills. Possible answers appear here in red.

Before Reading:

• What do I think this book is about?
- *I think this book is about Costa Rica.*
- *I think this book is about the beaches of Costa Rica.*

• What do I want to learn about this topic?
- *I want to learn about the animals that live in Costa Rica.*
- *I want to learn about the activities people do in Costa Rica.*

During Reading:

• I wonder why...
- *I wonder why there are volcanoes in Costa Rica.*
- *I wonder why there are so many forests in Costa Rica.*

• What have I learned so far?
- *I have learned that San José is the capital of Costa Rica.*
- *I have learned that jaguars are the biggest wild cats in Costa Rica.*

After Reading:

• What details did I learn about this topic?
- *I have learned that Costa Rica is in Central America.*
- *I have learned that San José is more than 200 years old.*

• Read the book again and look for the vocabulary words.
- *I see the word **capital** on page 4, and the word **erupted** on page 18. The other glossary words are on pages 22 and 23.*

COSTA RICA

Costa Rica is a small country.

It is in **Central America.**

San José is the **capital** of Costa Rica.

The city is more than 200 years old.

San José

Most people in Costa Rica speak Spanish.

San José has a large market.

Shoppers buy food, clothes, and other goods there.

Costa Rica has many forests.

They cover more than
half of the country's land.

These forests are important to Earth.

They take in a gas called **carbon dioxide**.

Factories and cars put out carbon dioxide as they burn fuel.

They put out oxygen that people and animals breathe.

Rain forests are home to many animals.

Scarlet macaws fly
from tree to tree.

Jaguars hunt in the dark.

They are the biggest
wild cats in Costa Rica.

Jaguars hunt on land and
in water. They eat deer, fish,
and many other animals.

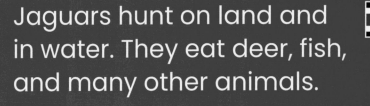

Costa Rica has beautiful waterfalls.

One is called La Paz.

Its name means peace.

Costa Rica has more than 60 volcanoes.

The Arenal volcano **erupted** many times.

Now it is quiet.

Beaches line the **coast**.

The sand is white and soft.

Costa Rica has so
much to see!

Glossary

capital (KAP-i-tl): The city where the government of a country or a state is located

carbon dioxide (KAAR-buhn dai-OX-side): A gas made when people and animals breathe out or when some fuels are burned

Central America (SEN-truhl uh-MEH-ruh-kuh): The region between Mexico and South America

coast (kohst): The land next to the ocean or sea

erupted (ee-RUPT-ed): Suddenly sent out lava, ash, rocks, or other material

rain forests (RAYN-faw-ruhsts): Dense, tropical forests that have large amounts of rainfall

Index

About the Author

Tracy Vonder Brink

Tracy Vonder Brink loves to visit new places. She has never been to Costa Rica, but she has read a lot about rain forests. She lives in Cincinnati with her husband, two daughters, and two rescue dogs.

Crabtree Publishing

crabtreebooks.com 800-387-7650

Copyright © 2022 Crabtree Publishing

Hardcover   978-1-0396-4460-1
Paperback   978-1-0396-4651-3

Printed in Canada/102023/CPC20231018

Published in Canada
Crabtree Publishing
616 Welland Avenue
St. Catharines, Ontario
L2M 5V6

Published in the United States
Crabtree Publishing
347 Fifth Avenue
Suite 1402-145
New York, NY 10016

Written by:Tracy Vonder Brink
Print book version produced jointly with Blue Door Education in 2023

Photo Credits: Shutterstock: DeLoyd Huenink: cover; Vlad Ispas: p. 3; mbrand85: p. 5; Inspired by maps: p. 7; Simon Dannhauer: p. 9; Cocos. Bounty: p. 10-11; Artem Oleshko: p. 10; gary yim: p. 12; G-Arbul: p. 13; Jamen Percy: p. 15; Dmitry Burlakov: p. 17; Bos11: p. 18-19; Tami Feed: p. 21

Library and Archives Canada
Cataloguing in Publication
Available at the Library and Archives Canada

Library of Congress
Cataloging-in-Publication Data
Available at the Library of Congress